Saul was the king of Israel, but he disobeyed God and so it was time to choose a new king. God asked the prophet Samuel to find someone to take his place.

There where plenty of big, strong, tall and good-looking men to choose from. But God picked a young shepherd to be the next king. His name was David.

God saw David's heart, and that he wanted to please God. Samuel anointed David with oil, but David still had many things to learn before becoming king.

David spent his days in the fields with the sheep. He was a good shepherd, caring and gentle. This was an important quality to have as a king, learning how to serve and be faithful.

David also sang of God's love and care. "The Lord is my shepherd and I have everything that I need. He makes me to rest in green pastures..."

David also knew how to be brave and courageous, another important quality for a king. Being a shepherd gave him lots of practice with this.

When wild animals came close to hunt for their favorite meal, David used his sling to scare them away. He spun it around and around, aimed, and then let the rock fly.

King Saul was very unhappy and moody at times. The king's advisors sent for David. "Come and help calm down the king with your beautiful music!" they said.

So David played the harp and sang and this helped to help cheer up the king. David also became best friend with the king's son, Jonathan.

For many years, there was constant war between the Isrealites and Philistines. David's older brothers were soldiers in Isreal's army.

One day a giant showed up with the Philistines army. His name was Goliath and he was huge. So big and strong that no one could even pick up his heavy sword.

Every day Goliath would shout, "Choose a man to fight me! If he wins, then we will be your slaves. But if I win, then you will be our slaves!"

**But no one dared to even get close. He was too big and scary.
But one day, David came by and heard Goliath's challenge.**

"If no one will fight him, then I will!" David said. The soldiers were in shock and Goliath thought it was funny. "This is going to be too easy. I'll just squash him." Goliath laughed.

The king offered David his armor, but David said, "I have a big God inside of me. I don't need this armor."

David collected some pebbles and prayed for God to give him courage. David was just a boy, but with God on his side, he was bold.

One pebble now found his home in David's sling and then took its biggest ride ever; around and around until it became topsy dizzy.

The stone flew and hit Goliath right on the forehead, and he came tumbling down! The Israelite army cheered, while the Philistines ran away.

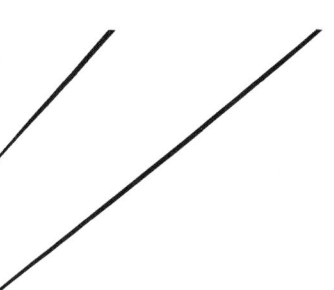

David became a hero that day. But he knew that it was because of God's power and strength. "Praise be to God that gives us the victory this day!" David said.

David grew up and went on to win many more battles. He also got married and had children. And finally he became the new king of Israel.

**David was a good king who loved God and loved his people.
He was caring and faithful just as he had been with his sheep.**

Kind David also made some big mistakes, but he was sorry, and God forgave him and loved him anyway.

David was called "a man after God's own heart". That's because David's heart was fixed on God. David wanted nothing more than to please God.

David wrote many songs of praise to God, and we still sing some of them today. You can find them in the Bible, in the book of Psalms.

Published by iCharacter Ltd. (Ireland)
www.icharacter.org
By Agnes and Salem de Bezenac
Illustrated by Agnes de Bezenac
Copyright 2015. All rights reserved.

Copyright © 2015 by iCharacter Ltd.. All rights reserved. No part of this book may be reproduced in any form or by any electronic or mechanical means, including information storage and retrieval systems, without written permission from the publisher or author, except in the case of a reviewer, who may quote brief passages embodied in critical articles or in a review.

Printed by BoD in Norderstedt, Germany